Food for Knapsackers

Good food is important to the success of any trip, and the knapsack trip is no exception. Increased weight is not required, nor is extra time for cooking, but one does need special knowledge and skill. Several Sierra Club knapsackers with a love of good food and an aversion to heavy packs have experimented with practical methods of serving appetizing, well-balanced meals. The ideas developed were then tested on Sierra Club summer trips. The results are presented in this book, with the hope that they will enable the beginner to serve adequate meals and the experienced knapsacker to enjoy them more.

The principles on which food planning is based are explained in considerable detail, both as a guide for individual experimentation and to facilitate the use of the new quick-cooking, dehydrated foods. Detailed instructions are given for both small and large groups, and include planning and organizing, cooking and cleaning up afterward. Also included are a master food list, recipes, sample menus and equipment lists; as well as suggestions for snow camping and other types of trips on which "going light" is an advantage.

Food for Knapsackers

and Other Trail Travelers
by Hasse Bunnelle
with Winnie Thomas

The Sierra Club, founded in 1892 by John Muir, has devoted itself to the study and protection of the nation's scenic and ecological resources — mountains, wetlands, woodlands, wild shores and rivers. All club publications are part of the nonprofit effort the club carries on as a public trust. There are 35 chapters coast to coast, in Hawaii and Alaska. Participation is invited in the club's program to enjoy and preserve wilderness everywhere. Address: 1050 Mills Tower, San Francisco, California 94104; 250 West 57th Street, New York, New York 10019; or 235 Massachusetts Avenue N.E., Washington, D.C. 20002

Copyright © 1971 by the Sierra Club.
All rights reserved.
Library of Congress catalogue card number 74-162395
International Standard Book Number: 87156-049-6

Second printing.

Designed and produced by Charles Curtis and printed in the United States of America by the Guinn Company. Illustrated by Sims Taback

Food for Knapsackers is published in cooperation with the Sierra Club Foundation.

Preface

As the smoke from many motors fills the air and hides
the view from the patio — and water from the faucet
becomes a mixture devised by the chemical industry —
increasing numbers of urban dwellers are seeking in the
mountains and deserts the space, clean air and clean
water denied them at home. Some travelers are content
to view the passing landscape from an automobile
window, and to see more country in less time. A growing
number prefer to go on foot into the wilderness and wild
areas, taking food and shelter on the backs of pack
stock, or carrying it in packs on their own backs. The
latter we know as knapsackers or backpackers, a breed
which has increased rapidly within the Sierra Club and
other outing organizations during recent years.

Pack boards — originally frames of wood on which
blankets, food and clothing were lashed — were used by
trappers and other early adventurers into the wilderness.

Knapsacking for fun, as a way to get into roadless country for the sheer pleasure of enjoying nature in its original form, is relatively new. Week-end trips began among some of the more stalwart Sierra Club members in the late 1930's, and in 1938 the club began to sponsor knapsack outings of one- and two-week duration.

Food for the early trips was limited largely to cereals, and canned goods, although some gourmets preferred for week-end trips such items as steaks, green salads and wine. Such foods are still popular for short and easy week-end trips, but for longer and more difficult week-end outings, and for all outings of a week or longer, weight *is* important.

The Knapsack Subcommittee of the Outing Committee has compiled the knowledge of many experienced cooks in an effort to provide its leaders with light weight, easily prepared foods for summer outings. We have used slide rules to figure exact amounts of food, spent endless hours arguing the relative merits of one herb or another, and have subjected countless week-end knapsackers to trial recipes. Out of it all has come Winnie's Master Food List — an easy way to decide how little food is needed for a given number of people, menus and recipes to guide beginners and to give experienced knapsackers new ideas. The simplest food becomes a treat when eaten in the gentle drift of campfire smoke. The pleasure is heightened if the mixture in your Sierra Club cup is tasty and well prepared.

H.B.

Acknowledgements

Most helpful were the many Sierra Club knapsackers who, by their enthusiasm for experimental meals and their eagerness to see this booklet in print, have kept the project under way.

Bob Braun, Chairman of the Knapsack Subcommittee of the Outing Committee, was responsible for the original project of preparing knapsack information in written form. Three food leaflets were part of a series that was available for several years. The first leaflet was written by Betty Christeler, although earlier instructions had been prepared by Ramona Wascher and others for a knapsack training course given by the San Francisco Bay Chapter. Subsequent leaflets, as well as this book, represent the development and elaboration of earlier plans and ideas.

Betty Osborn, Secretary of the Knapsack Subcommittee, has done more than anyone else to stimulate and

7

facilitate the writing of a single publication on knapsack cooking.

Wesley Bunnelle served as the Number One guinea pig for new recipes, and acted as consultant on many aspects of the planning and preparation of the booklet.

Paul and Peggy Grunland assisted in compiling much of the information for the original Master Food List, and Gertrude Cawley, formerly dietician for a clinic where one of us was employed, gave helpful assistance with the technical aspects of nutrition. Neil Anderson suggested variations for cooking under snow-camping conditions. Tom Amneus suggested variations for desert trips. Additional recipes and suggestions have come from Nancy Cutter, Eunice Dodds, Robert V. Golden, Margo Gwinn, Ketty Johnson, John Jencks and others.

Many leaders of summer knapsack outings kept detailed records of the food they carried, listing items that were in short supply and those that went unused. This information formed the basis for revisions of the Master Food List, and greatly increased the authors' confidence in its reliability.

Historical information about the Sierra Club cup was provided by William E. Colby, the club's first outing leader and committee chairman, and third president.

The book spent some of its final days of preparation in the hands of Fred Gunsky, editor and a knapsacker who enjoys good food.

To all of these we wish to express our sincere appreciation, for without them *Food for Knapsackers* would not be in print.

W.T. and H.B.

Contents

The Sierra Club Cup

The First Sierra Club outing — the High Trip —
was organized and led in 1901 by William E.
Colby, who was to serve for 36 years as chairman
of the Outing Committee, for 49 years as a
member of the Board of Directors, as the club's
third President, and its Honorary President until
his death in 1964.

Will Colby searched for several years after the
first High Trip for a suitable tin cup to use on the
trips. He wanted a cup strong enough for daily
rough usage and designed to nest for packing
purposes. In 1905, members of the Appalachian
Club who joined the Sierra Club outing to Mount
Rainier brought with them cups which suited Mr.
Colby's specifications exactly. Cups of the same
design, with the club name embossed on the
bottom, were ordered for the club and have been
in use ever since — a badge worn proudly on the
belts of thousands of hiking and climbing members. A change of suppliers was necessary in 1949,
and the present ten ounce stainless steel cup was
adopted. The club now supplies cups embossed
with the Sierra Club name to members, and the
same cup, without the name, to several mountaineering equipment stores.

1. Principles of food planning

Enough to eat but nothing to throw away, minimum weight and bulk, no spoilage, meals that are easy to prepare and tasty and leave one satisfied until the next meal — these are the things to keep in mind when planning food for a knapsack trip. The principles of food planning, once learned, leave the cook free to improvise new and tastier dishes — or quicker and easier ones.

Adequate nutrition. Both the quantity and the type of food are important, especially on trips of more than a few days. Unless otherwise specified, suggestions in this booklet are for trips of the type represented by Sierra Club summer knapsack outings. This usually means fairly strenuous activity, with groups of 15 to 25 people — more men than women, of ages ranging from mid-teens to late middle age with the young adult group predominating. Experience has shown that under such circumstances an average diet of about 2,800 to 3,000 calories per person per day is satisfactory for the first three or four days, after which an additional 400 or 500 calories per day are needed. Most people lose weight at first, then appetites increase more nearly in proportion to the energy being expended. On one-week trips, food requirements for an average group can be met — without fishing — by carrying one and one-half pounds per person per day of dehydrated food.

Some groups have reported that they ate adequately on one pound per person per day, but this involves the risk of going a bit hungry if there are too many large appetites, if the trip is unusually strenuous, or if the weather is colder than anticipated.

Differences in the weight of food for different types of group composition are discussed in the section on preparation of menus and food lists (p. 25).

The principal difference in planning food for two or three people instead of for twenty or thirty is that averages are less dependable, and it becomes more important to consider individual appetites and tastes.

A balance between carbohydrates, proteins and fats is important to provide sustained energy, especially after breakfast and lunch. Carbohydrates (sugars and starches) are the most quickly available, energy from proteins becomes available later and is more lasting, and fats are the most slowly utilized. Providing adequate carbohydrates is rarely a problem, but care is needed to assure sufficient protein and fat, especially for breakfast. Suggestions as to how this can be accomplished are given in the next chapter, in the section on the preparation of menus and food lists. If meals are well planned, there will be little craving for candy and other between-meal snacks.

Minerals and vitamins usually present no problem, especially if most crackers and cereals are of the whole grain variety. Vitamin C, however, may be deficient unless dehydrated citrus fruit juice or some other beverage known to contain this vitamin is served daily. Vitamin C is important in maintaining resistance to infections. Tablets of ascorbic acid (Vitamin C), 50 milligrams or more per person per day, may be substituted for citrus juice.

Salt is important, since correct salt balance is essential to a feeling of well-being. The amount of salt lost in perspiration varies considerably between individuals and changes with acclimatization. During strenuous activity, especially in hot weather at the beginning of a trip, most people want and need more salt than can be added to food without spoiling its flavor. However, tastes and the need for salt vary, so a salt shaker should be readily available at mealtime. Since too much salt is as undesirable as too little, each person needs to be alert to his own craving for salt and adjust his intake accordingly. Other signs of salt deficiency are excessive fatigue, headache, stomach cramps, and diarrhea. Many hikers carry salt tablets to take with water when symptoms occur.

Sufficient water to prevent dehydration is also essential. Substantially more water is usually lost during a day's hike than is replaced, regardless of how much has been available along the trail. Many people do not drink enough fluids during the twenty-four hours to replace this loss unless a considerable amount of water is combined with their food. Lemonade is a refreshing means of increasing fluids for lunch or when camp is made early. Soup is excellent for breakfast or dinner, and a generous supply of hot water for beverages should be available for both meals.

Light weight and low bulk. Light weight and low bulk are of primary concern on all but very short trips. To achieve this, keep the water content of foods to a minimum, eliminate heavy packaging materials, and avoid excessive air inside packages. Use dehydrated foods, repackage most of the food in polyethylene bags — tin cans add 15 to 25 per cent to the weight of the contents, and cardboard packages add 5 to 10 per cent — and avoid low-density items such as corn flakes or soda crackers. Another way to reduce weight is to increase the use of fat, such as bacon grease or margarine, because fat has over twice as many calories per ounce as protein or carbohydrate. Even so, the diet probably will contain a lower proportion of fat than usual, since there are few rich sauces and desserts. Unless freeze-dried products are available and within one's budget, meat is the most difficult food to provide in variety without carrying a substantial amount of excess weight in the form of water and tin cans. Good quality freeze-dried meats have been developed and are available in many large markets. Freeze-dried foods also can be obtained from mountaineering supply firms but still are more expensive than fresh or canned foods. If both minimum weight and minimum price are important, adequate high quality protein can be provided by using additional powdered milk, powdered eggs, and dry cheese. For a more detailed discussion of dehydrated foods, see the section at the end of this chapter.

No spoilage. It is important to choose foods that keep well under trip conditions. Avoid items labeled "keep under refrigeration" except for use during the first day or two. A former knapsack staple now in this category is

16

chipped beef. It has become almost impossible to find the dry, salty variety except in small glass jars. The plastic packages of thinly sliced, partially dried beef stored in refrigerated counters do not keep well in warm knapsacks. Most processed cheeses spoil quickly and melt at pack temperatures, and milk chocolate can turn into a sticky mess.

Easy preparation and appetite appeal. Meals that are easy to prepare and tempting to eat are the other major requirements. Lunch is the most difficult meal to make appetizing, since nearly everything must be hard and dry and the choice of food is somewhat limited. However, with careful planning it is possible to offer reasonable variety. Variety may also be increased by serving different lunch materials on different days. Detailed suggestions for lunches are included in the section *Preparation of menus and food lists.* When lunches are carried individually it is important to keep different types of food separate. Five or six pint-size polyethylene bags to go inside a larger bag of the same material are light in weight and practical for this purpose.

Dinner, also, is more appetizing if it presents variety in flavor, texture and color. For example, cream of mushroom soup, macaroni and cheese, and vanilla pudding would be discouragingly alike in appearance and texture. Vegetable soup, macaroni and cheese, and a fruit gelatin dessert would be a much more appetizing combination. Herbs and spices add only a few ounces to the load and can make a substantial contribution to the menu. They should be used with discretion unless the cook is certain of individual tastes.

Adaptation to requirements of a trip. Special requirements of the trip should be considered. For days when

18

long hours are to be spent hiking, both breakfast and dinner menus should consist entirely of foods that are quick and easy to prepare. When the pace is leisurely, many cooks enjoy trying their skill at more complicated dishes.

Other situations that require special plans are camps above timberline or on snow, and travel through areas without drinking water. The section, *Modifications for other types of trips* (p. 52) gives details as to how this can be done.

Co-ordination of menus and cooking utensils. An easily overlooked aspect of planning is the need to match menus and cooking utensils. Although, for example, the same pot can be used for soup and later for heating water, it is important that the menus and utensils be cross-checked in advance of the trip.

Reasonable availability of foods. Foods that are easy to obtain are a great convenience. Supermarkets and neighborhood stores have an increasing variety of quick-cooking, dehydrated food. On long trips, however, it is an advantage to have greater variety of fruits, vegetables and dehydrated or freeze-dried meats than such stores ordinarily carry. Oriental markets have some useful dried foods, and most mountaineering supply firms will send catalogs and fill orders by mail. The *Master Food List* (p. 57) includes suggestions as to where unusual items can be obtained.

Notes on dehydrated foods. The Incas of Peru freeze-dried meat, fish, potatoes and other foods by exposing them to the night cold of the Andes. Thus preserved, the foods could be stored for later use and reconstituted in boiling water. Today's explorer of the wilderness can fill his pack with a wide variety of lightweight foods, many of them already mixed and seasoned, requiring only the additon of hot water to turn them into palatable meals. Experiments with' survival foods for the armed forces and for the astronauts have been responsible for the development of much compact and lightweight food. As a result of increased popular demand, several processors of fruits, vegetables and meats have prepared them in dehydrated or freeze-dried form. Briefly, dehydrated foods are prepared by placing dried fruits and vegetables in a vacuum chamber until all moisture is removed. Freeze-drying is done by placing frozen foods in a vacuum chamber until the moisture has been removed. In freeze-drying, mineral salts remain within the tissues of the food and are not drawn to the surface with evaporating juices, as happens when drying is done by vacuum without freezing. The resulting foods retain their shape, flavor and color and usually weigh 20 to 30 per cent of their original weight. Such foods will keep indefinitely if sealed against air and moisture, and are easily prepared. Both dehydrated and freeze-dried foods may be reconstituted in a few minutes by adding a small amount of water.

A variety of freeze-dried or dehydrated items may be obtained from mountaineering supply houses by mail order, and an increasing number may be found in local markets. Ease of preparation and storage has increased the home use of such foods, and made them more readily available to the camp cook. An entire meal may be prepared with dry packaged mixes from supermarket

shelves. In addition to popular soups from many countries, mixtures of various meats, soy protein, vegetable, starch, and seasoning have been introduced. Such mixes are usually heavy on starch and light on meat, so additional freeze-dried meat may be added, or a cream soup or pudding served with the meal. Dessert mixes are widely available in many attractive forms, some to be baked and others only to be chilled.

Items packaged for one or two persons are to be found in mountaineering specialty shops and other stores. Look for fish chowder, concentrated food tablets, jerky, freeze-dried fruits and vegetables, hash, stew, and soup; bacon bars, freeze-dried ham, meat balls, and beef or pork patties. Cereals are packaged for two, as are small packets of tea bags, and fruit drinks. There are tubes of preserves, small packages of rye bread, chocolate malt tablets, peanut butter, and cheese spreads packaged for individuals or for two.

Check the shelves of supermarkets, visit health food stores and the gourmet sections of department stores. Write to mountaineering supply houses for catalogs if there is no store nearby. So many new items are being produced each year that no published list could be complete. The partial list of suppliers in this book will provide a helpful start.

2. Procedure and equipment

Preparation of menu and food lists. A menu pattern has been developed for Sierra Club summer knapsack trips that meets the criteria discussed in the preceding chapter. *Breakfast* usually consists of (1) stewed fruit or citrus juice, (2) cereal cooked with margarine and milk, *and* (3) ham, bacon or scrambled eggs (dehydrated). Dry cereal may be available for those who do not like the cooked variety, and pancakes or biscuits may be substituted for cereal when time permits. Milk is prepared to use with the cereal and in beverages, and a supply of instant coffee, tea bags and chocolate mix is set out on a convenient rock or log, to be mixed with water kept boiling on the fire. *Lunches* and *snacks* consist of a variety of crackers and dark bread, dry sausages, several varieties of dry cheese, nuts, hard candies, semi-sweet chocolate, dried fruits, hard cookies and packaged lemonade or other fruit drinks. For

dinner, there is soup, a main dish containing meat or meat substitute and a starchy ingredient such as rice, noodles or potatoes, a vegetable (added to the soup or main dish), dessert, and the same beverages that were served for breakfast.

The *Master Food List* and the recipes given in the next chapter provide a basis for preparing food lists for such meals. The *Master Food List* is organized by meals and by categories of food for each meal, except for beverages and certain staples (milk, margarine, sugar, etc.), which are listed for the trip as a whole. The list gives the amount of each item of food that is required per person per meal or per person per day in the case of staples and beverages. These amounts are correlated with the recipes although there are occasional minor differences when quantities in some recipes are rounded off to standard measurements.

The food list for a trip for breakfast and dinner ingredients can be planned by either of two methods. The safer and more precise method, especially for beginners, is to prepare a complete set of menus for all meals. Then list all ingredients except beverages and staples that will be required for each meal. Calculate the required amount of each ingredient by multiplying the weight in ounces given in the *Master Food List* by the number of people in the party. Except for very small groups, it is usually easier to measure by weight than by volume. This requires a scale that measures up to about 20 pounds, with calibrations to a quarter-pound or less. If a postal scale is available, the weight method is practical even for two or three people. This method of preparing exact menus reduces the danger of forgetting essential ingredients, or taking too much or too little, or of ending the trip with a day or two of poorly balanced, unappetizing meals.

A somewhat different method, often preferred by those with experience, requires less pre-trip planning and allows greater freedom to adapt menus to the mood and tempo of the day. Decide in advance how many times each food is to be served on the trip, but not what specific recipes will be used or what combinations of food will be served together. For example, in planning food for dinners, list as many servings of meat or meat substitute as there will be days on the trip. Do the same for soup or soup base, starchy foods, vegetables and desserts. A similar procedure can be followed for breakfasts. The amount of each food item is calculated from the *Master Food List* as before, but must be multiplied by the number of times the food is to be served.

The food list for lunches should be planned for the trip as a whole. Determine the amount of food in each major category by multiplying the requirements per person per day (as given in the *Master Food List*) by the number of man-days. The number of man-days is the number of people in the party times the number of days the trip is to be out. For example, calculate the total required weight of crackers and bread, then select individual items so that their weight equals this total.

Prepare the lists of staples and of beverages by multiplying the amounts in the *Master Food List* by the number of man-days. The amounts of these items are fairly standard except that the amount of sugar will vary with the number of times syrup or jam is to be served. The *Master Food List* allows enough sugar for one or the other twice a week. Make necessary changes on the basis of amounts in recipes to be used.

Prepare a shopping list by adding together items that appear more than once on the food lists. Except for food that is purchased in bulk, the size of packages must be taken into consideration. Package sizes change so frequently that little attempt has been made to take them into account, either in the recipes or in the *Master Food List.* Consequently, there will be left-overs, either when repacking or on the trip.

The amounts of food per person per meal or per day in the *Master Food List,* when used for the types of menus suggested, are fairly reliable for one-week trips with average groups — a few more men than women, and with ages ranging from late teens to late middle age. If there are many adolescents, assume that each will eat about 25 per cent more food than is listed. This can be provided by adding extra luncheon foods, powdered milk, and cocoa mix. There should be about eight ounces of such additional items per boy or girl per day. If there are men only, add 4 oz. per person per day to the basic amounts. For two-week trips, add 4 oz. per person per day for the second week.

Packaging food to carry. Repackaging saves weight, makes it possible to carry the exact amount of food needed, and to pre-mix foods that will be used together. For example, it is convenient to pre-mix skimmed and whole milk, cocoa mix and milk for hot chocolate, or vegetables and dry seasonings for a main dish. Canned foods such as nuts and citrus fruit crystals should be repackaged. With the latter, be sure to include the desiccator and to use double plastic bags. Bags of food are much easier to carry than round or square containers.

Package foods for each meal and for each day

together when possible. Mix dry ingredients and seasonings for stews, or for powdered eggs, milk and seasonings. Powders require double bags, each bag securely fastened with a rubber band or a wire-twist fastener after the air has been pushed out of it. Labels indicating the contents, the quantity, and special instructions are easily read if slipped between the inner and outer bag, or printed on the inner bag with a felt marking pen. Double bags, tied separately, are especially important for greasy foods such as cheese, margarine, or bacon. Liquids such as french dressing or salad oil can be put in polyethylene or other hard plastic bottles. The bottles become rancid after two or three trips and should be discarded. Maple, vanilla and other flavorings are available in such small bottles that the extra weight of the glass is negligible, but they must be carefully wrapped to avoid breakage. Herbs and spices may be carried in 35 mm. film cans, labeled on a slip of paper scotch-taped around the can. Place such seasonings together in a plastic bag which will be bulky but light. If foods are bagged for small groups by the day, staples such as milk, salt, and beverages may be distributed equally throughout the packages in order that such supplies will not all be used too early in the trip. Cold days require more hot drinks than do warm days, so if more cocoa is used on one day than on another, it won't matter.

For large groups and longer periods of time, a packing party provides an easy way to package the trip food. Three or four people can package all of the food for twenty people for a week within a few hours. Provide scales, quart and pint plastic bags, rubber bands or wire twists, and a plastic scoop for shoveling milk, egg and other powders into the proper sized bags. Label the bags with felt pens before filling. Mark packages of food with the day and meal for which it is planned. This will save time and confusion on the trail.

Stoves. Cooking on small one-burner stoves allows a better choice of camp sites. The stoves can be moved into shelter away from cold wind or rain, and are cleaner and quicker to use than a wood fire. Certain rules must be followed for success and safety with stoves: 1) Learn to operate the stove *before* starting the trip. 2) Two stoves are more convenient, even for a small group, since one stove is much too slow. 3) Set the stoves in a location protected from wind. Use a light metal windscreen. Stoves do not operate in wind. 4) Fill stoves *before* starting a meal. Gasoline is dangerous and must be kept away from fires and operating stoves. Fill only while the stove is cold — never during the cooking process. 5) Use *only* white gas, and carry it in tightly capped containers, wrapped in double plastic bags, in an outside pocket of the pack or in the pack of a hiker who is not carrying food. 6) Figure the fuel requirements carefully before starting the trip. Gasoline weighs 1.5 pounds per quart. For example, the fuel requirement for a seven-day, two-man trip has been calculated at a little over two quarts, so two quarts with two stoves filled would be enough.

In addition to gasoline stoves, there are alcohol, kerosene and butane stoves. A can of solid fuel may also be used by placing the lighted fuel under an elevated wire grill on which the pots are placed. Here again, two stoves are more convenient and faster than one. Kerosene is less inflammable than gasoline, but is harder to light, smelly, and greasy. Alcohol is heavier and less efficient than gasoline. One pound of alcohol has about

half the heating value of one pound of gasoline. Butane has about the same heating value as gasoline, but must be kept in pressure cartridges. Before purchasing a stove, look carefully at all types, and question the users of various stoves as to their experience and recommendations.

Cooking equipment. For cooking the type of meals suggested in this manual, a set of three or four pots, preferably with covers, a griddle or frying pan, and a plastic mixing bowl are sufficient. The largest pot should contain at least one pint per person, with a second pot of the same size or slightly smaller. Also needed on most trips are two or three large spoons with handles long enough to rest on the rims of the pots, a wire whisk for mixing milk, a pancake turner, a sharp knife, a can opener if there are tin cans, and a pot grabber if there are pots or pans without handles. Handles should be of metal or wood because plastic, when placed too close to the fire, melts into an awkward blob. A light-weight wire grill is almost a necessity for supporting the cooking pots and for broiling fish. For large groups (10 or more people) it is worth the extra weight to add one or two ladles for serving, a slicing knife, a one-quart plastic measure, an oven mitt for lifting pots, canvas or leather work gloves for handling hot rocks when breaking camp, and a large sheet of medium-weight plastic on which to spread out the food supplies and with which to cover them in case of rain. A painter's drop cloth is good for this purpose, or plastic sheeting can be bought by the yard in most department stores.

For dishwashing, a metal or hard plastic sponge is convenient for scrubbing pots and pans, although sand can serve in an emergency. With large groups, a long-handled brush protects the dishwasher's hands from

the relatively long immersion in hot water. Soap should be used rather than detergent because it is less detrimental to the water supply. Bars that float are most convenient, although soap powder may be carried in an 8 oz. wide-mouthed plastic bottle, well labeled so it will not be confused with powdered milk. Soap is removed from the water as a scum by combination with dissolved minerals, and is also decomposed by bacteria. Most detergents are not affected by such purifying and remain in the water. The cumulative effect can be an acrid taste to city water, or suds in a park fountain. In mountain lakes and streams, detergents are injurious to fish and other aquatic life, and should not be used.

Cooking equipment should be carried in cloth or plastic bags to protect the pack and other gear from soot and abrasion. For equipment used by small groups (fewer than 10 people) the bags may be made from muslin or light-weight, closely-woven nylon. For larger equipment, cotton twill, denim or flour sacking is suitable.

For parties of six or less, good light-weight nested pots with frying pan covers can be purchased from mountaineering specialty firms. If economy is more important, a practical and flexible set can be assembled from the light-weight aluminum sauce-pans available in most variety and hardware stores. Such pans usually nest well, but have the disadvantage of fixed handles. Covers can be purchased separately, but for odd pots, pie plates are preferable since they will serve other purposes. Three pie tins, two stacked as a double bottom, the third overturned as a top, may be used as a small dutch oven for baking in the coals. For frying, a heavy-weight cake pan with a pot grabber or pliers, a light-weight aluminum frying pan, or a magnesium griddle is satisfactory. A small wire cake grill is suitable for the cook fire. For large groups, nested pots with bail handles and large griddles and grills can be obtained from mountaineering specialty firms or from restaurant supply houses. The total weight of cooking equipment can be kept to one pound or less per person if care is taken in its selection. Suggested cooking equipment lists for large and small groups are included in Chapter 4.

A Sierra Club cup, or its equivalent, and a spoon and pocket knife are sufficient for eating equipment. Cautious travelers will carry duplicates. Take a salad fork if you are not going extra light.

Cooking procedures. It is wise to decide in advance who is to be responsible for cooking. In small groups, the arrangement may be an informal one, but one person should be in charge, with others gathering wood, carrying water and washing dishes.

On Sierra Club summer knapsack trips, which usually have twenty to twenty-five members, it is customary for the leader to divide the group into cook crews of three or four people each. An experienced person is assigned to each crew as the chief cook. Crews are numbered, and rotate responsibility for a dinner and the following breakfast. The next crew cleans up, and the members have only themselves to blame if they start cooking with dirty pots. Luncheon supplies are usually put out after breakfast for each member of the party to make his own selections. Replenishing lunches every other day has been a satisfactory arrangement on many trips, although some leaders prefer to make this a daily routine.

Establishing the wilderness kitchen. In selecting a campsite, the availability of a good location for cooking is of primary importance. In areas where downed wood

is wet from much rain, is scarce or nonexistent, small gasoline, alcohol, butane, or solid fuel stoves must be used. For the conservation of both wood and scenic values and because of increasingly heavy travel in wilderness back country, such stoves should be used more frequently by groups of all sizes.

The first requirement of a good site is *safety* from fire hazards. Fire should be built only on mineral soil, sand or rock and should be located a safe distance from trees and brush. A fire built on the partially decomposed organic debris found in all forested areas can smoulder for days after it appears to have been extinguished. Then it can spring into flame when no one is around to prevent disaster. To minimize the danger that sparks will reach anything that can ignite, several feet of bare surface should surround all camp or cook fires. A second requirement is *preservation of the wilderness* from signs of human use. Plan in advance for removal of all visible evidence of the fireplace and other kitchen operations, unless the site is a regularly used campground. Several types of location that are safe from fire hazards should not be used because of damage to esthetic values. This includes damp mountain meadows, which will remain scarred for many years, and bare expanses of rock that can remain black for generations. *Convenience for cooking, comfort for the cooks,* and *scenic surroundings* are the remaining considerations.

The ideal location is a moderately open, relatively flat area with dirt, sand or rock not more than a few inches below the surface. Water for cooking and for drowning the fire should be reasonably accessible. An adequate supply of down wood should be readily available, unless fuel has been carried in. Dead wood should not be cut or

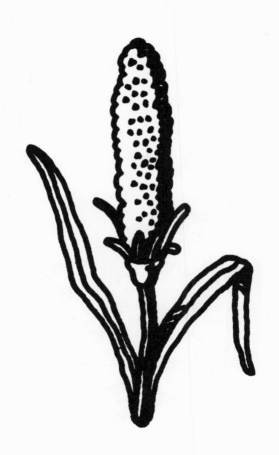

broken off trees or standing snags, for such trees are an integral part of the wilderness scene. A selection of medium-sized rocks is useful for building the fireplace, and large flat rocks make good kitchen tables. Protection from the wind may be important. Shade from a hot evening sun is desirable, but morning sun is nearly always welcome. Each camper will have his own criteria for the choice of scenery.

If a new fireplace must be built, scrape away the combustible debris from an area about six feet in diameter. Then scoop out a small trench, carefully saving the sand or dirt that is removed. Fifteen to eighteen inches long, four inches deep and eight inches wide is about the right size. Build up two parallel rows of flat rocks, one on each side of the trench, to support the grill. It should be just high enough to allow convenient feeding of the fire, usually about eight inches. A *small* fire does less damage than a large one, is easier to cook on, and requires less firewood. Cookfires, even small ones, will usually burn better if built against a rock. However, this practice mars the natural appearance of the rock by blackening it and by destroying its crystalline structure so that it flakes and crumbles. A thin, flat rock may be placed between the fire and the back rock, or it may be used alone.

Before lighting the fire, a moderate pile of good down wood, one or two inches in diameter, should be gathered, broken into usable lengths and stacked within easy reach of the cook. Paper is not essential for starting a fire but is a convenience. Lacking or scorning paper, carefully arrange a few small dry twigs to form a wigwam and light with a match held near the center. A bit of pitch at the top helps, especially in damp weather.

Larger twigs should be ready to add at the strategic moment, and finally sticks from the regular supply. Starting a fire in the rain from a single match is an achievement to be remembered. Most cooks want everyone else to leave the fire strictly alone. If a pot does boil over there is no cause for alarm. The accident automatically lowers the flame and the cook has only to replace water and readjust the fire.

A group should make only one fire, since even the best job of obliteration is less than perfect, and wood supplies need to be conserved. After dinner, remove the grill, add more wood, set a pot of water to heat at the fire's edge, and the campfire is ready, with hot beverages as an added attraction.

All fires should be completely extinguished with water before they are left unattended, even for a short time. If this is not done, an unexpected gust of wind can fan the embers into flame and scatter sparks beyond the cleared area, with the possibility of a forest fire.

Storing food in camp. Protecting the food supply in camp is usually quite simple. The most common hazard is rain from unexpected storms. In most mountain areas, whenever the group leaves camp, or if clouds threaten at night, the food should be covered with polyethylene or other waterproof material. This also gives some protection from chipmunks and other small marauders, although food is safer from them if suspended from the branches of a tree.

Bears can be a problem, especially in or near national park campgrounds. Most people trust to luck in the back country, but if a bear does raid camp, the damage is impressive. However, the worst food raiders in the back country are deer, marmots and burros. At night, it is a

good precaution to rig a bear alarm by stacking pots and other metal gear on top of the food. When disturbed by a bear or other animal, the resulting clatter is enough to waken a camper sleeping nearby, who can then chase away the animal by shouting and banging pots and pans. The bear alarm should then be reassembled for the next encounter. In bear country, it is not safe to store food in backpacks near bed sites.

A safer method of protecting food, especially when no one is in camp, is known to its enthusiasts as "bear-bagging." A length of about 1/8" diameter nylon rope is tied to a small rock and thrown over a sturdy limb 15 feet or more above the ground and as far out along the limb as is feasible. All food not in tin cans is packed in a bag about the size of a pillow-case. Such a bag will hold about 40 pounds of food. The bag is tied securely to one end of the nylon rope, and is hoisted up as high as possible. The free end of the rope is then tied to a nearby tree trunk or branch.

Cleaning up, Sierra Club style. As soon as cooking starts, the trash and garbage problem arises. Camp trash is made up partly of combustibles and partly of noncombustibles. Leftover food, plastic bags, and paper are the principal combustible refuse. Such materials are consumed completely if fed to the fire in small amounts. In large amounts, they do not burn well. Polyethylene and other plastics tend to smother the fire and to produce foul odors. All plastic items except small bags should be packed out. Quantities of leftover food, if thrown in the fire, produce clouds of smoke, tax the wood supply, and remain largely unburned. Most leftover food should be scattered in inconspicuous places well away from the camp and trail, where it will quickly be consumed by insects, birds and mammals.

All noncombustible garbage must be carried out for disposal. Tin cans should be burned in the fire after both ends have been removed. They may then be smashed flat and stowed in polyethylene bags. Do not wait until the morning of departure to burn accumulated cans and other garbage, for neither the burning nor the cooking will be effective. Burning is best done after each meal.

Aluminum foil and foil containers should be packed directly into discarded polyethylene bags. Foil is not completely consumed by fire but breaks into small pieces which are nearly impossible to separate from the ashes. These bright bits of metal do not weather away but remain for years as telltale evidence of the camp. Many food items such as milk, dehydrated soups and gum are packaged in paper or plastic, underneath which will be found a layer of foil. Such containers should be carried out unburned. Pouring spouts of cartons are usually of aluminum. They should be removed and added to the collection of noncombustibles.

The best way to minimize the amount of trash, as well as to reduce the total weight carried in, is to remove most of the food from its containers before the trip, and to repack it in polyethylene bags. If glass containers are carried into the wilderness, they must be carried out. The section on *Packaging food to carry* (p. 31) gives procedure for repackaging.

Dishwashing is a chore enjoyed by few but of importance to all. In small groups pots may require only rinsing or scrubbing in warm water. Soap and a metal scouring sponge are useful for stubborn dirt or scorched pans. Individual eating utensils are usually cared for by their owners. In large groups esthetic and sanitary

considerations require that all cooking utensils be washed in hot suds and rinsed well in hot water. This can be done in the larger pots. For individual eating utensils, a pot of hot, soapy water with a long-handled brush for scrubbing, and a second pot of boiling water for rinsing should be provided. This method affords protection against one of the main ways in which infections spread through large groups of people who camp together.

Both dishwater and rinse water should be dumped well away from streams or lakes, preferably in brush or among scattered rocks where it will not run back into the water supply, and where the food debris will not be noticeable.

When camp is broken, every effort should be made to leave the campsite clean and inviting. A virgin area should be returned as nearly as possible to its original condition and appearance. The fireplace is the most difficult artifact to dispose of, but the following method is a good one. First, let the fire burn down as low as possible. This will reduce the accumulated coals to a small volume of ashes. Then drown the fire in its trench with plenty of water and stir with a stick until the ashes are cool enough to be felt with the hand. Dismantling the fireplace is next. A pair of work gloves make the handling of hot rocks much easier and safer. Rocks should be returned, black side down, to their original positions, or buried in sand or soil in a natural way. Next, cover the ashes in the trench with the dirt previously saved for this purpose. Stamp and smooth the surface to conform to the surrounding area. Then give it a coat of sand or ground litter that will blend with the undisturbed cover. Excess firewood should be scattered, preferably in brush.

There is a deep sense of satisfaction and achievement in the knowledge that one has traveled through an area without leaving perceptible traces — and in harmony with the spirit of the wilderness.

Modifications for other types of trips. Many of the ideas suggested in this book are useful on other types of trips especially when compact loads and quick, easy cooking are important — such as on burro trips, some boat trips, snow trips, and even car camping.

Food for snow trips is much the same as for summer knapsacking, but with a few important differences. Cooking is usually restricted to small one-burner alcohol, gasoline or butane stoves, and even these are difficult to use in a snowstorm or blizzard. Cooking equipment for a party of five should consist of one or two stoves, a container of fuel with at least one pint per stove per day, and two covered pots, each of about four-pint capacity. A larger pot and wire grill may be carried if there is hope of finding down wood for an open campfire. Pots that are black on the bottom absorb heat better than those with polished surfaces, and an asbestos sheet wrapped around a pot conserves heat. If natural shelter from wind is not available, dig a small snow cave or set the stove in the entrance of a tent. If a tent is used, have good ventilation because carbon monoxide is deadly. It is also important to avoid fire hazards, since most tent materials are inflammable. If wood can be found and there is not too much wind, a small campfire saves liquid fuel and is warm and cheerful. A wire grill can be balanced on the wood, but pots need careful watching to avoid upsets. On well-packed snow, one location usually lasts long enough to cook a meal.

When cooking on a one-burner stove, one-dish meals

should be planned, with a second pot used to melt snow and heat water. Food must be quick-cooking to conserve fuel. A good breakfast might consist of quick oats, fortified with margarine, raisins and powdered milk, served with brown sugar. Heat water for coffee, tea or chocolate. Dinner can be any soupy stew containing meat, cereal or potato, a vegetable, and fat. Suggested ingredients are pre-cooked rice, dehydrated mashed potato, freeze-dried or canned meat, bouillon cubes, vegetable flakes, and margarine. Suitable recipes are Spanish rice or corned beef stew with the substitution of mashed potato for potato slices, and with additional water in both dishes. For details, see the section *Recipes*. In addition to the usual beverages, hot fruit gelatin does double duty as dessert. A ski-touring favorite when cooking must be kept to a minimum is a mixture of equal parts of powdered milk or chocolate milk, instant malted milk and wheat germ. The mixture is stirred into hot water, with butter or margarine added if available. This makes a surprisingly adequate and satisfying meal. The total weight of the mixture per person per meal should be about eight ounces, if nothing else is eaten. Another possibility for emergencies is to carry ready-to-eat survival foods, such as MPF (Multi-Purpose Food).

Since there are times when no cooking is possible, it is important to carry more immediately edible food than on most knapsack trips. At least half the total supply should be in this category. Cold weather stimulates the appetite for rich, spicy items such as fruit cake or packaged mince meat. These may be added to the foods suggested for knapsack lunches. Peeled oranges carried in a plastic bag are delicious for quick energy and to quench thirst when there is no water.

Adequate fluid intake is especially important, because the body can lose a great deal of moisture in cold weather without noticeable perspiration, especially at high altitude. If no water is available, snow may be allowed to melt in the mouth. This is a slow but satisfactory way of getting a drink of water. Melt snow in camp for beverages if the stoves can be used long enough. Hot tea is a satisfying drink and makes otherwise cold meals much more palatable. When melting snow, melt a layer of water on the bottom of the pot before filling it with snow. Dry snow *does* scorch.

Dishwashing on a snow trip is a simple procedure. Fuel should not be wasted melting dishwater. Scrape the dishes as clean as possible, scrub them with hard-crusted snow, and don't look too closely at the result. Otherwise, the usual cleanup procedures should be followed insofar as is possible under snow conditions. All noncombustible materials, such as tin cans, glass and aluminum foil should be carried out.

When camping above timberline, cooking procedures are essentially the same as for snow camping. Cooking must be done on gasoline, alcohol or butane stoves unless wood has been carried up. Even then, economy in its use dictates meals of the one-pot variety.

Knapsacking in desert country requires modification of the types of food carried. Some light-weight dehydrated foods may be carried if a known source of water will be available. Foods with a high water content, such as oranges, should be carried, especially for lunches. Canned juices are a refreshing source of fluid, and other canned foods are quicker and easier to prepare than the usual knapsack fare — and save precious water and wood supplies. Avoid foods such as ham or corned beef, which increase thirst. Wood is unavailable in some desert areas, and stoves may be carried as for snow camping.

Because of the need to carry water — four quarts per person per day including juices at all times when away from reliable sources — knapsacking weights are higher than is necessary in mountain regions where water is readily accessible.

Whatever the means of transportation or the character of the area traversed, food can be both nutritious and delicious. We hope this book will stimulate an increasing number of knapsack cooks to consider food an integral part of the pleasure of wilderness travel.

3. Master food lists

The amounts of food in this list are for an average group of 15-25, and are for the first week of a trip.

Per Person Per Meal

BREAKFASTS: Fruits	Net weight in Ounces	Approx. Vol. in Cups	Calories	Comments
Applesauce, instant*	1.0		105	
Apples (vacuum-dried)*	1.0		105	
Apricots (vacuum-dried)*	1.0		100	
Peaches (vacuum-dried)*	1.0		100	
Prunes (vacuum-dried)*	1.0		105	
Dried fruit (regular)	1.4		105 (approx.)	
Raisins or currants	0.4	1/8	30	Cook with cereal.
Grapefruit crystals*	0.8		75	Popular and easy.
Orange juice crystals*	0.8		85	Popular and easy.
Cereals				
Fine-ground (e.g., Wheatena or Wheat Hearts)	1.5	1/3	140	Some good high-protein cereals are available. Check labels for comparative analysis.

Rolled oats	1.5	1/2	160	Quick-cooking cereals are often preferable.
Grapenuts or other compact dry cereal	1.5	1/3	150	Dry cereal is popular.
Pancake mix	2.0	1/2 (scant)	200	More will usually be eaten if available.
Biscuit mix	2.2	1/2	300	
Wheat germ		1 or 2 T.		Adds flavor and nutritional value to biscuits, cereal, etc.
Meat and egg				
Freeze-dried ham slices	0.8		120 (approx.)	
Smoked pork shoulder (boneless)	1.6		150	Uncut rolls keep about two weeks.
Ham (boneless)	1.6		150	
Bacon	1.6		290	Unsliced keeps best. Use fat if possible.
Eggs, powdered	1.0	1/3	170	0.5 oz. = 2-1/2 T. = 1 egg.

LUNCHES AND SNACKS:

(Total Weight—9 ounces per person per day.)

Crackers and bread

Triscuits	1.6	220
Various hard dry crackers		180 (approx.)
Pumpernickel bread		100	The heavy dark type keeps well.

Bagels

Meat

Dry sausage	1.1	120	Landjaeger, Lebanon bologna, dry salami and Thuringer are good.
Jerky	2.0	100 (approx.)	
Ready-to-eat smoked pork shoulder or ham	1.1	100	Buy boneless, unsliced type. Be sure it is already cooked.
Dried shrimp	1.1	80 (approx.)	Available in Oriental markets.
Freeze-dried cooked meat slices	1.1	100 (approx.)	Reconstitutes in a few minutes.

Dry cheese	1.6	170	Cheddar is most popular. Swiss, Provolone and Monterey Dry Jack keep better.
Nuts	1.0	170	Mixed nuts are good. Peanuts are cheapest and usually least popular.
Peanut butter	1.0	200 (approx.)	Very popular. Repackage in plastic tubes or cartons.
Hard candy	0.7	80 (approx.)	Fruit-flavored, coffee blacks, peppermints and butter balls are suitable.
Chocolate (semi-sweet)	1.0	130	Do not carry milk chocolate in warm weather.

Cookies	0.6		
Fig bars		60	
Hard cookies		90	Most popular.
Fruit			
Regular dried	1.3	100	Peaches, apricots, prunes and raisins are usual favorites.
Vacuum-dried	1.0		Except for apples, vacuum-dried fruit is better if soaked for 5 min. or more before eating. It can then be carried in a plastic bag.
Apple pie slices		105	
Apricots		100	
Peaches		100	
Prunes		105	
Fruit-ade mix	0.5	50	Try brand before trip.

Dehydrated potato slices	1.4		140
Bulghour wheat (e.g., Ala)	1.6	1/4	160
Dehydrated yams	2.0		
Vegetables			
Spinach flakes*	0.4	2/3	35
Cabbage flakes*	0.8	1/2	70
Onion flakes*			
Tomato flakes*			
Tomato paste			
Dried mushrooms			
Desserts			
Gelatin dessert (e.g., Jello)	1.0	1/3 pkg.	100
Instant pudding	1.3	1/3 pkg.	130
Cheesecake			
Graham cracker crust mix			

Spinach flakes* through Dried mushrooms: } See recipes for amounts.

Dried mushrooms — Can be purchased in Oriental or Italian markets.

Cheesecake, Graham cracker crust mix — See package for amounts.

Packaged topping mix	0.4		Use as whipped cream.
Fruit cocktail mix (vacuum-dried)	1.0	100	
Fruit (vacuum-dried)	1.0	100	
Fruit (regular dried)	1.3	100	
Hard cookies	0.6	90 (approx.)	Serve with fruit or gelatin.

—————— Per Person Per Day ——————

Beverages			
Instant coffee	0.15		Groups vary widely in the proportion of coffee, tea or chocolate preferred. These amounts are averages.
Instant tea	0.15		
Tea bags	1-1/2 bags		
Instant cocoa mix	0.9	1/4 (scant) 120	May be mixed with milk before the trip. See recipe (p. 87) for proportions.
Fruit-ade mix	0.5		Check label for addition of vitamin C.

Staples

Instant non-fat milk powder	1.0	1/3	100	The milk powders may be mixed before re-packaging. The mixture has better flavor if mixed in advance.
Whole milk powder	0.5	1/8	80	
Milk with low fat content (powder)	1.0	1/3	110	
Sugar, white	1.2	1/6	130	More sugar is needed if syrup, jam or chocolate sauce is served more than twice a week.
Sugar, brown	0.5	1/16	50	For cereal, syrup, etc.
Margarine	1.2	1/6	250	*Most calories per ounce* of any food on the list.
Salt	0.2			

69

Item			Amount for 12-day, 20 man trip (240 man-days)	Comments
Flour	10 to 20	0.1 to 0.2		Used for thickening gravy and frying fish.
Corn meal	10	0.1		If desired for frying fish.

Condiments

Item	Amount	Comments
Pepper	4 oz.	
Garlic powder	1/2 oz.	
Mustard powder	1-1/2 oz.	
Oregano	1/2 oz.	
Basil	1/2 oz.	Select on the basis of personal preference.
Tarragon	1/2 oz.	
Parsley flakes	1 oz.	
Celery salt	3 oz.	
Chili powder	2 oz.	
Curry powder	1-1/4 oz.	
Cinnamon	2 oz.	
Vanilla	1 oz.	
Maple flavoring	2 oz.	Sometimes available in tablet form.
Bouillon cubes or powder	20 cubes or packets	

Miscellaneous

Matches	1 large box	
Toilet paper	8 rolls	Not enough to use as Kleenex.
Soap (floating type)	3 large bars	
Plastic freezer bags, 1 pint size	200 bags	For lunches (5 or 6 per person) and for re-packaging.
Plastic freezer bags, 8" x 3" x 15" size	200 bags	For lunches (1 per person) and for repack-aging.

*Can be obtained in stores specializing in mountaineering supplies. See *partial list of suppliers.*

Calories were calculated from tables in Johnson, H.J., *Bridges Dietetics for the Clinician* (5th Ed.), Philadelphia 1949 and Bowes, Anna and Church, Charles F., *Food Values of Portions Commonly Used*, Philadelphia 1951.

Note: The occasional use of brand names is for purposes of clarity and does not imply the recommendation of any particular product.

4. Recipes and suggestions

Useful Information

1 Sierra Club cup = 10 oz. = 1-1/4 standard cups
1 gallon (gal.) = 4 quarts (qt.) = 16 cups (c.) standard
1 tablespoon (T.) = 3 teaspoons (t.)
1 pound (lb.) of water or sugar = 2 c. = 16 oz.
1 cube margarine = 4 oz.

1. Cooking time increases with altitude. At 8,000 feet elevation cooking time is approximately double that at sea level, although this factor varies for different foods. Many dehydrated foods are precooked, so the cooking time is essentially the time required for reconstitution and heating, regardless of the elevation.
2. When soaking vacuum-dried foods, put the food in the pot and add water—two volumes of water to one

volume of food. Do not fill the pot with water and then add the food, as there will be excess water to pour off and juices will be wasted. This of course does not apply to soups or stews where extra water will be needed.

3. When making soup, if the volume is insufficient, *do not* add more water without adding more soup mix, bouillon cubes, vegetables or margarine, or soup will be watery and flavorless.

4. With starches such as rice and potato, check the recipes or *Master Food List* for the amounts to use for servings. Be particularly careful with rice—it is easy to prepare too much.

5. The quantity per serving of prepared dehydrated foods such as soup required for hungry hikers eating the kinds of meals suggested in this book may vary considerably from the quantities per serving listed on most packages. Plan in terms of the *Master Food List* or the *Recipes* rather than from the package instructions. Allow one pint of water per person for soup or other drinks.

6. Margarine, if added to the water before cereal is added, helps prevent it from sticking to the pot.

7. Add margarine to dehydrated or freeze-dried meats (usually prepared without fat except for corned beef), as additional seasoning and food value. Add it to drained noodles and macaroni, if they have been cooked separately from the rest of the main dish. See the *Recipes* for quantities. Bouillon cubes may also be added—beef cubes or soup base to beef, chicken cubes or soup base to chicken or turkey, margarine or chicken to fish.

8. If a snow-bank is available, make gelatin and let it cool in the snow. Snow may also be used to replace

the cold water used in the recipe. Use in approximately equal volume to boiling water.

9. For packaged main course mixes with protein, starch and vegetable, use at least three ounces per person, dry weight.

10. Mix milk with powdered eggs, pudding, etc. at home at the time of repackaging.

11. Add dry seasonings to dry ingredients whenever possible. The food will taste better and be easier to prepare if all such ingredients and seasonings are mixed and packaged at home.

Recipes

Cooking times are for approximately 8,000 feet elevation.

Measurements are standard units.

Milk powder as specified in the following recipes refers to instant non-fat milk powder or to a mixture of three parts by weight of non-fat milk powder with one part of whole milk powder. This is a ratio 4 to 1 if measured by volume.

Season food well, but avoid strong or unusual seasonings unless you are certain the entire group likes them.

FOR BREAKFAST

Fruit	*For Five*	*For Twenty*
Stewed fruit		
Water	2 c.	2 qts.

Vacuum-dried fruit or	5 oz.	20 oz.
regular dried fruit	7 oz.	28 oz.
Sugar (optional)	1/4 c.	1 c.

Add the fruit to cold water and simmer about 10 minutes for vacuum-dried, or 20 minutes for regular dried fruit. Add sugar and more water if needed. Double the sugar for apricots. Nutmeg and brown sugar improve any stewed fruit mix.

Citrus fruit mix.

Water	3-2/3 c.	3-2/3 qt.
Fruit crystals	4 oz.	16 oz.

Add the crystals to cold water, stirring until dissolved.

Apricot jam

Water	1-1/2 c.	1-1/2 qt.
Apricots, vacuum-dried,	4 oz.	16 oz.
or regular dried	6 oz.	24 oz.
Sugar	8 oz. (1 c.)	32 oz. (1 qt.)

Prepare the same as stewed fruit. Cook down if too juicy. Stir continuously after adding the sugar to prevent scorching.

Main dishes

Fine-ground quick-cooking cereals (Wheat Hearts, Wheatena, Protein Plus, etc.)

Water	6 c.	6 qt.
Cereal	8 oz.	32 oz.
	(1-1/2 c.)	(1-1/2 qt.)
Milk powder	4-1/2 oz.	18 oz.
	(1-1/2 c.)	(1-1/2 qt.)

Margarine	3 oz.	12 oz.
	(3/4 cube)	(3/4 lb.)
Salt to taste		
Seedless raisins or chopped dates (optional)	2 oz.	8 oz.

Add the margarine to the water. When boiling, add the mixed cereal and milk powder. Stir vigorously. Salt to taste. Cook 5 to 10 minutes, adding more water if necessary and fruit if desired.

Rolled oats

Water	6 c.	6 qt.
Rolled oats	8 oz.	32 oz.
	(3-1/2 c.)	(3 1/4 qt.)
Milk powder	4-1/2 oz.	18 oz.
	(1-1/2 c.)	(1-1/2 qt.)
Margarine	3 oz.	12 oz.
	(3/4 cube)	(3 cubes)
Seedless raisins or chopped dates (optional)	2 oz.	8 oz.
Salt to taste		

Prepare as above, *stirring as little as possible* to avoid sticking.

Pancakes

Pancake mix	10 oz.	40 oz.
	(2 c.)	(2 qt.)
Milk powder	2 oz.	8 oz.
	(1/2 c.)	(2-1/2 c.)
Water	1-1/2 c	1-1/2 qt.

| Margarine or bacon fat | 4 oz. | 16 oz. |
| | (1/2 c.) | (2 c.) |

Add water to the pancake mix and powdered milk, stir in melted fat and cook on lightly greased griddle. Avoid too hot a fire.

Egg pancakes

Pancake mix	6 oz.	24 oz.
	(1-1/4 c.)	(1-1/4 qt.)
Powdered eggs	4 oz.	16 oz.
	(1-1/2 c.)	(1-1/2 qt.)
Milk powder	2 oz.	8 oz.
	(1/2 c.)	(2-1/2 c.)
Water	1-1/2 c.	1-1/2 qt.
Margarine or bacon fat	4 oz.	16 oz.
	(1/2 c.)	(2 c.)

Prepare as for regular pancakes. The batter should be a little thinner.

Syrup

Brown sugar	8 oz.	32 oz.
	(1 c.)	(4 c.)
Water	3/4 c.	3 c.

Bring the sugar and water to a boil. White sugar and maple flavoring may be substituted.

Biscuits

Biscuit mix	11 oz.	Not usually
	(2-1/2 c.)	practical for
Milk powder	1 oz.	more than
	(1/3 c.)	ten.
Water	3/4 c.	

Egg (optional)	1 oz.
	(1/3 c.)
Wheat germ (optional)	1 oz.
	(1/3 c.)

Mix the dry ingredients. Add water, mixing with as little stirring as possible. Dough should be very stiff. Pat into a well-greased 9″ cake or frying pan. Cook the bottom over a low fire until light brown, testing by lifting an edge of the biscuit. Tilt the pan at a 45° angle in front of a fairly hot fire. This can be done by resting one edge of the pan on a flat rock with the back supported by a larger rock. Heat on the surface of the biscuits should be such that one's hand can be held there only momentarily. The pan will need to be rotated once or twice to bake evenly. Baking should take 10 or 15 minutes.

For a delicious breakfast, serve biscuits with margarine, apricot jam and fried smoked pork. Quantities are not listed for 20 people because the usual griddle is not large enough.

Hashed brown potatoes

Water	2 qt.	2 gal.
Potato slices	8 oz.	32 oz.
Margarine	2 oz.	8 oz.
	(1/2 cube)	(2 cubes)

Salt and pepper to taste

Add potato slices to cold salted water and boil 30 min. or until soft. Drain well and fry in margarine until brown, adding parsley flakes if desired.

Scrambled eggs

Powdered eggs	5 oz.	20 oz.
	(1-3/4 c.)	(7 c.)
Milk powder	(1/4 c.)	3 oz.
		(1 c.)
Water	2 c.	2 qt.
Salt and pepper to taste		

Add water to the egg and milk powders. Stir until fairly smooth. Season and cook over a low fire, stirring just enough to insure uniform thickening, or fry on a greased griddle. For variety, add diced cheddar cheese, diced cooked ham, parsley flakes, tarragon, basil, sweet marjoram, or curry powder. Crumble in a bacon bar or two.

Mix egg and milk powder and add dry seasonings at the time of repackaging individual meals. The flavor will be better.

Trout

Trout can be baked, broiled, boiled, and fried to a gourmet's satisfaction provided a few hints are followed in their preparation.

1. Keep trout cool while fishing. Pack in moist grass in creel as they are caught, and clean them promptly. Avoid carrying them in plastic bags as they will get too warm, fats turn to oils, and the entire flesh will be permeated with a fishy odor.

2. Trout up to about 12" are best either fried or boiled. Larger fish should be baked or broiled and filleted (boned).

3. If frying, remember that bacon grease has a strong flavor that can overcome the delicacy of a fresh trout. Margarine, butter, or cooking oil is better.

4. Well-prepared trout should fall away from the bones readily. In boning, the meat is cut lengthwise from the bones gently and swiftly. It is best to see it done first, then learn through experience the proper method.

5. Cold fried trout are delicious for lunch and can be easily kept overnight if allowed to cool, then wrapped in wax paper. On extended trips into the back country, cold fried trout provide an excellent variation for the trailside lunch.

6. Salt and pepper are sufficient seasonings for breakfast and lunch. For dinner, there are other possibilities. See page 108.

Beverages

Milk
FOR CEREAL OR COFFEE

Instant skimmed milk	3 oz. (1 c.)	12 oz. (1 qt.)
Whole milk powder	1 oz. (1/4 c.)	4 oz. (1 c.)
Water	2 c.	2 qt.

Mix the milk powders, stir in water and beat until smooth. The flavor improves with standing for half an hour or more. Some groups will not use this much milk.

FOR DRINKING

Add to the above	1 cup water	1 quart water

Or, use milk powder packaged by the quart (the kind with low fat content). Mix by the quart as needed. A few drops of vanilla in the milk helps the flavor. For those who like it, a tablespoon of coffee will also improve a cup of milk.

Hot chocolate	*(One cup)*	*(One gal. – 16 c.)*
Instant cocoa mix	2 T. (level)	8 oz. (2 c.)
Milk powder	1/4 c.	12 oz. (1 qt.)

Mix the dry ingredients and gradually add hot water, stirring until smooth.

Mocha, a mixture of half cocoa and half coffee, with milk and sugar added to the hot water, is very popular.

Lemonade

Lemon powder	4 oz.
Sugar	16 oz. (2 c.)
Water	2 gal.

Mix the lemon powder with sugar and sprinkle into the water while beating vigorously. Lemon powder absorbs moisture so rapidly that the package should not be opened until ready to use.

FOR DINNER

Soups

Vegetable soup

Water	2 qt.	8 qt. (2 gal.)
Mixed vegetable flakes	2 oz.	8 oz. (3 c.)
Onion flakes	1/2 oz.	2 oz. (1 c.)
Margarine	2 oz.	8 oz.
	(1/2 cube)	(2 cubes)
Bouillon cubes or	5	20
beef base	1 oz.	4 oz.
	(1/4 c.)	(3/4 c.)

Salt and pepper to taste

Add vegetable flakes to the cold water. Boil for about

20 minutes, adding other ingredients and salt and pepper to taste.

Package soups

Many good dehydrated mixes are available and may be used separately or in combination. Good combinations are green pea and onion soup, or cream of mushroom and chicken noodle. Use the number of packages required for the amounts of water given above for vegetable soup.

Clear soup

Water	2 qt.	8 qt. (2 gal.)
	(1/2 gal.)	
Rice or barley	1-1/2 oz.	6 oz.
	(1/3 c.)	(1-1/2 c.)
Bouillon cubes or beef	8	32
or chicken base	1-1/2 oz.	6 oz.
	(1/3 c.)	(1-1/2 c.)

Salt and pepper to taste

Mix ingredients and boil until the rice or barley is soft. Barley requires about an hour.

Cream soup

Any soup can be made cream-style by adding milk powder, approximately 1-1/2 cup (4 oz.) for five people, or 1-1/2 qt. (1 lb.) for twenty. Mix to a thin paste with cold water and add to the soup just before serving. Use slightly less water than usual in the original soup.

Minestrone

| Water | 2 qt. | 2 gal. |
| Freeze-dried ground | 5 oz. | 20 oz. |

beef *or* fresh ground chuck	20 oz.	5 lbs.
Macaroni, shells or wagonwheels	5 oz.	1 lb.
Tomato flakes	2 oz.	8 oz.
Onion flakes	1 oz.	4 oz.
Mixed vegetable flakes	4 oz.	16 oz.
Celery flakes	1/2 oz.	2 oz.
Garlic powder	1 t.	2 T.
Basil	2 t.	2 T.
Margarine	2 oz.	8 oz.
Beef bouillon	3 cubes	12 cubes

Salt and pepper to taste

Soak meat and vegetable flakes 15 to 20 min., add margarine and bouillon cubes, and bring to boil. Add macaroni and seasonings and cook until meat and macaroni are done. Add basil and other herbs 5 min. before serving.

Other vegetables may be substituted for those used. Try corn, peas, or beans or all three instead of mixed flakes.

This may be used as the main dish, or as a soup. Fresh beef can be used at the roadhead, or the first night after a hot, hard hike. Good for the night when few fish have been caught.

Chicken soup plus

Water	2 qt.	2 gal.
Soy flour	1/2 c.	2 c.
Brewer's (nutritional) yeast	1/4 c.	1 c.
Dry milk	1/2 c.	2 c.

Bouillon cubes (chicken)	3 cubes	12 cubes
Margarine	2 T.	8 T.
Parsley flakes	1 T.	4 T.
Onion flakes, chives	1 T.	4 T.

Mix dry ingredients, stir into water and bring to a boil. Add margarine, bouillon cubes and simmer. Add leftover ham or chicken bits. Add seasonings a few minutes before serving.

Salads

"Fresh" vegetable salad

Mixed vegetable flakes	2 oz. (3/4 c.)	8 oz. (3 c.)
French dressing	1-1/2 oz. (3 T.)	6 oz. (3/4 c.)

Cover the vegetable flakes with cold water and soak for 30 minutes. Drain well and marinate in French dressing.

Cabbage slaw

Cabbage flakes	2 oz. (3/4 c.)	10 oz. (3 c.)
Onion flakes	1/2 oz.	2 oz.
Sour cream sauce	3 oz.	12 oz.
Dill weed	1/2 t.	2 T.
Lemon juice	1 T.	4 T.
Salt to taste		

Cover flakes with water and soak until water is absorbed and vegetables are barely crisp. Mix dry sour cream sauce, dill weed, and salt until extra water is

absorbed and the mixture covers flakes like thin cream. Add lemon juice and mix well.

Vegetable-gelatin salad

Gelatin dessert (lime-, lemon- or apple-flavored)	1 pkg. (3 oz.)	5 pkg. (15 oz.)
Water (boiling)	1-3/4 c.	2-1/4 qt.
If very cold stream is not available, use only	1-1/2 c.	1-3/4 qt.
Mixed vegetable flakes	2 oz. (3/4 c.)	8 oz. (3 c.)

Dissolve the gelatin in boiling water and set in a stream to chill, weighting the cover with a rock. Soak the vegetable flakes as above, drain well and add them to the gelatin. Chill until set, allowing 1 to 2 hours for entire process. (See Item 8, page 75)

Vegetables

Cabbage

Water	6 c.	6 qt.
Cabbage flakes	4 oz. (2 c.)	16 oz. (2 qt.)
Margarine	1 oz.	4 oz. (1 cube)

Salt and pepper to taste

Add the cabbage flakes to cold water, salt and boil about 15 minutes. Drain and season with pepper and margarine.

Spinach

Water	6 c.	6 qt.

Spinach flakes	2 oz. (3 c.)	8 oz. (3 qt.)
Margarine	1 oz.	4 oz.
		(1 cube)

Salt and pepper to taste

Add the spinach flakes to cold water, salt and bring to a boil. Drain and season with pepper and margarine.

Green beans
Water, to cover

Green beans, dehydrated	2 oz.	1/2 lb.
Salt	1 t.	1 T.
Butter	1/2 cube	3 cubes

Soak about 20 min. Bring to boil, cover, cook 15 min. Drain well. Add butter, salt and pepper.

Add slivered almonds for a new taste treat.

Green peas
Water, to cover

Green peas, freeze-dried	2-1/2 oz.	10 oz.
Margarine	1 oz.	4 oz.
Basil (optional)	1 t.	4 t.

Salt and pepper to taste

Soak about 10 min. Bring to boil, cook about 10 min. Drain well. Add butter and seasonings.

Corn
Water, to cover

Corn, freeze-dried	2 oz.	12 oz.
Margarine	1 oz.	4 oz.
Comino (optional)	1/2 t.	2 t.

Salt and pepper to taste

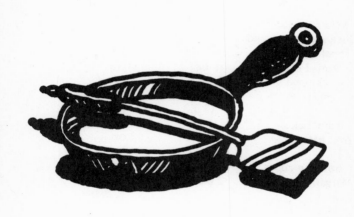

Flour	1 T.	4 T.
Chopped raisins	2 T.	8 T.
Chopped almonds	1/4 c.	1 c.
Bouillon cube, beef	1	4
Onion flakes	4 T.	1 c.
or minced		
onions, medium	4	16
Garlic cloves, minced	1	4
Margarine (or butter)	2 T.	2 cubes
Curry powder	3 t.	4 T.
Ginger	1 t.	4 t.
Salt and pepper to taste		

Add freeze-dried meat, flakes, and seasonings to water and let soak 10 min. Bring to boil and add margarine, raisins, almonds, and bouillon cubes. Add flour to thicken sauce. Let simmer 15 min. or until meat is done. Serve over hot rice.

If using fresh meat, cook onion and garlic in fat, add meat and brown lightly. Blend in flour, add seasonings and other ingredients. Bring to a boil and simmer, covered, 15 minutes. Serve over hot rice.

Italian spaghetti

Water	3 c.	3 qt.
Freeze-dried ground beef or canned roast beef	5 oz.	20 oz.
	12 oz. (1 can)	60 oz. (5 cans)
Tomato flakes	3 oz. (1-1/4 c.)	12 oz. (5 c.)
or tomato paste	6 oz.	24 oz. (4 cans)
Dried mushrooms	1/2 oz.	2 oz.
Onion flakes	1/2 oz. (3 T.)	2 oz. (3/4 c.)

Margarine	3 oz.	12 oz.
Basil	1/2 t.	2 t.
Garlic powder	1/4 t.	1 t.
(to taste)		
Spaghetti	8 oz.	32 oz.
Parmesan cheese	1 oz.	3 oz.
(grated)		

Salt and pepper to taste

For the sauce, break the mushrooms into bits and soak 10 minutes. Add the beef, mushrooms, vegetables, seasonings and margarine to the cold water, bring to a boil and simmer about 20 min. Add more water if too thick. (5 pkgs. of spaghetti sauce mix for 20 people may be substituted for the mushrooms, onion and seasonings.)

Boil the spaghetti in salted water about 20 minutes, drain and serve with the sauce and Parmesan cheese. If there is a shortage of pots, double the water and cook the spaghetti in the sauce.

Corned beef stew

Water	2 qt.	2 gal.
Potato slices	5 oz.	20 oz.
(dehydrated)		
Onion flakes	1 oz.	4 oz.
	(1/3 c.)	(1-1/2 c.)
Cabbage flakes	3 oz. (2 c.)	12 oz. (2 qt.)
Margarine	3 oz.	12 oz.
Corned beef	12 oz.	60 oz. (5 cans)

Salt and pepper to taste

Add the potato and other vegetables to the cold water, bring to a boil, add margarine, seasonings and corned beef. Boil for about 40 minutes.

Beef Stroganoff

Freeze-dried beef, chunks or ground	5 oz.	20 oz.
Bouillon cubes	2	8
Onion flakes	1 oz.	5 oz.
Dried mushrooms	1 oz.	5 oz.
Sour cream sauce	4 oz.	16 oz.
Milk powder	4 oz.	16 oz.
Parsley flakes	1 T.	5 T.

Salt and pepper to taste

Cut beef chunks into smaller pieces, break mushrooms into bits, add onion flakes and soak in water to cover for 15 or 20 min. Bring to a boil and simmer until meat is done. Mix sour cream and milk with 3 cups cold water until smooth, and add to meat mixture. Add seasonings and mix well. Bring to a boil and cook until mixture is a medium-thick sauce, adding a small amount of hot water if it is too thick. Serve over rice or noodles.

Tamale pie

Water	2 qt.	2 gal.
Mushrooms	2 oz.	8 oz.
Freeze-dried ground beef or canned roast beef	5 oz.	20 oz.
	12 oz.	60 oz. (5 cans)
Tomato flakes	4 oz. (1-1/2 c.)	16 oz. (6 c.)
or tomato paste	6 oz. (1 can)	30 oz. (5 cans)
Onion flakes	1 oz. (1/3 c.)	4 oz. (1-1/2 c.)
Green pepper flakes	1-1/2 T.	1/2 oz. (1/3 c.)
Chili powder	1 T.	1 oz. (1/4 c.)

Garlic powder to taste	1/4 t.	1 t.
Margarine	3 oz.	12 oz.
Corn meal	8 oz.	32 oz.
	(1-1/2 c.)	(6-1/2 c.)

Salt and pepper to taste

Break mushrooms into bits and soak 10 minutes. Add the beef, mushrooms, vegetables and seasonings to the cold water and bring to a boil. Stir in corn meal, add margarine, and simmer for about 40 minutes or until the corn meal is done. Add water if necessary to maintain a mush-like consistency.

Spanish rice

Water	2 qt.	2 gal.
Freeze-dried ground beef or canned roast beef	5 oz.	20 oz.
	12 oz.	60 oz. (5 cans)
Tomato flakes	3 oz.	12 oz. (5 c.)
	(1-1/4 c.)	
or tomato paste	6 oz. (1 can)	24 oz. (4 cans)
Onion flakes	3/4 oz.	3 oz. (1 c.)
	(1/4 c.)	
Green pepper flakes	1 T.	1/2 oz.
		(1/3 c.)
Margarine	3 oz.	12 oz.
Rice	8 oz.	32 oz.
	(2-1/4 c.)	(2-1/4 qt.)
Garlic powder to taste	1/8 t.	1/2 t.

Salt and pepper to taste

Add the meat and vegetables to the cold water and bring to a boil. Add the margarine, seasonings and rice. Simmer for 5 to 10 minutes.

Beef hash

Water	2 qt.	2 gal.
Potato slices	8 oz.	32 oz.
Onion flakes	1/4 oz. (1-1/2 T.)	1 oz. (1/3 c.)
Corned beef or freeze- dried ground beef	12 oz. (1 can) 5 oz.	60 oz. (5 cans) 20 oz.
Salt and pepper to taste		

Add all ingredients to the cold water, bring to a boil and cook about 40 minutes. Season, drain well and fry in margarine (8 to 12 oz.) until brown, or serve without draining as a stew.

Joe's special

Water	2-1/2 c.	2-1/2 qt.
Freeze-dried ground beef	4 oz.	16 oz.
Onion flakes	1/2 oz.	2 oz.
Spinach flakes	1-1/2 oz.	6 oz.
Powdered egg	3 oz.	12 oz.
Water	1/2 c.	2 c.
Basil	1/2 to 1 t.	1/2 to 1 T.
Garlic powder	1/8 t.	1/2 t.
Parmesan cheese (optional)	1 oz.	3 oz.
Salt and pepper to taste		

Add the meat and vegetables to the cold water and soak for 15 minutes. Mix the egg powder to a paste with the remaining water. Combine the mixtures and add seasonings. Cook over a low fire, stirring just enough to insure uniform thickening, or fry on a greased griddle.

(This can be prepared more quickly if all dry ingredients are mixed and repackaged at home.)

Boston beans

Water	6 c.	6 qt.
Precooked beans	10 oz. (2 c.)	40 oz. (2 qt.)
Onion flakes	1-1/2 T.	1 oz. (1/3 c.)
Brown sugar	2 T.	1/2 c.
Smoked pork shoulder	6 oz.	24 oz.
Mustard	1/2 to 2 T.	2 to 8 T.
Salt and pepper to taste		

Add the beans, onion, diced pork shoulder and brown sugar to the cold water. Bring to a boil, add salt, pepper and mustard to taste and cook about 40 minutes.

Chili beans

Water	6 c.	6 qt.
Precooked beans	10 oz.	40 oz.
Tomato flakes	2 oz. (3/4 c.)	8 oz. (3 c.)
Onion flakes	1/2 oz. (3 T.)	2 oz. (3/4 c.)
Freeze-dried ground beef or canned roast beef	3 oz. 12 oz.	12 oz. 36 oz. (3 cans)
Chili powder	1 to 2 T.	4 to 8 T.
Salt and pepper to taste		

Add beans, tomato, onion and beef to the cold water. Bring to a boil, add salt, pepper and chili powder to taste and cook about 40 minutes.

Rice and ham

Water	2 qt.	2 gal.
Smoked pork shoulder or ham	10 oz.	40 oz.
Parsley flakes	1 T.	1/4 c.
Chicken base or chicken bouillon	1/2 oz. 3 cubes	2 oz. 12 cubes
Onion flakes	1 T.	1 oz. (5 T.)
Precooked rice	8 oz. (2-1/4 c.)	32 oz. (2-1/4 qt.)
Margarine	2 oz.	8 oz.

Salt and pepper to taste

Cook the diced pork and the onion flakes in the water for 10 minutes. Add other ingredients, simmer for 5 minutes and let stand 5 minutes. Serve with applesauce. (See breakfast recipes.) One-half to one ounce of dried seaweed broken in bits and added to this recipe adds a delightful fresh flavor.

If trout fishing has been good, save the ham planned for this dish. Slice and fry it for breakfast. The rice dish, with margarine or butter to season, goes well with trout. Broil or grill the fresh-caught fish and season with butter and lemon.

Golden (Bob) trout Parmesan

Prepare cheese sauce: In a small saucepan, or Sierra Club cup, heat about half a cube of margarine or the equivalent amount of cooking oil until it boils. Take off fire, stir in white flour slowly until the mixture has the consistency of loose cookie dough. Add hot water little by little, stirring constantly over fire until mixture is thin enough not to stick to the pan. Boil about one

minute to cook fat and flour; add a few spoonfuls of grated Parmesan cheese, stirring constantly. Add salt to taste and keep warm at the edge of fire.

Boil trout: Put a flat pan of water on fire and bring to a boil. Water should be just deep enough to cover fish, and may be seasoned lightly with salt, pepper, lemon, and parsley flakes if available. Place fish in boiling water for a few minutes until flesh on both sides of backbone can be easily removed. Bone fish, and serve with a light spooning of cheese sauce.

Baked ham

Ham, canned (5 oz. per person) (use 1 lb. or 3 lb. cans)	2 lb.	6 lb.
Mustard, dry	4 T.	16 T.
Cloves, ground	1 T.	4 T.
Apple or guava jelly	6 T.	1 pint

Place ham and juice in a shallow pan, or the bottom of a pot. Spread with seasonings that have been mixed at home. Bake covered until heated through and browned slightly. Serve with whipped yams, green beans with almonds, and pistachio pudding.

Chicken and dumplings

Water to cover		
Freeze-dried chicken or fresh chicken pieces	5 oz.	20 oz.
	3 lb.	12 lb.
Parsley	2 T.	1/2 oz.
Chicken bouillon	3 cubes	12 cubes
Margarine	2 oz.	8 oz.
Basil	1 T.	4 T.

sauce. If there is a shortage of pots, double the water in the sauce and cook the noodles in this before thickening.

Cream sauce

Water (boiling)	3 c.	3 qt.
Margarine	3 oz.	12 oz.
Milk powder	3 oz. (1 c.)	12 oz. (4 c.)
Flour	1/3 c.	1-1/2 c.

Mix the milk and flour. Stir in cold water until the consistency of a thin paste. Stir this into the boiling water. Add the margarine, salt to taste, and simmer for a few minutes.

Or, make a roux by adding flour to melted margarine, stirring until flour is cooked but not brown. Stir in salt and milk, and simmer until mixture reaches the desired thickness. Add more water if the mixture is too thick.

Turkey or chicken curry

Curry powder	1 T.	4 T.
Coriander (ground)	1 t.	4 t.
Cream sauce (see recipe above)	3 c. (approx.)	3 qt. (approx.)
Freeze-dried turkey or chicken *or* boneless turkey or chicken (cans)	4 oz.	16 oz.
	15 oz.	50 oz.
Rice (instant)	8 oz.	32 oz.
Margarine	2 T.	8 oz.
Salt to taste		

Add curry powder and coriander to flour and make a medium thin sauce. Add meat, heat to a boil and let simmer a few minutes until the meat is hot and sauce is well mixed with meat. If freeze-dried meat is used, soak 15 or 20 minutes before adding (with soaking water) to sauce. Let simmer until meat is done, mixing well. Prepare rice in boiling, salted water to which margarine has been added. Serve curry mixture over rice, with chutney and sambals.

Chutney

Fruit galaxy	6 oz.	1 lb.
Onion flakes	1-1/2 oz.	6 oz.
Brown sugar	2 oz.	8 oz.
Dry mustard	1 T.	5 T.
Garlic powder	1 t.	4 t.
Cloves (ground)	1/2 t.	3 t.
Cayenne	1/2 t.	3 t.
Turmeric	1 t.	3 t.
Ginger root, chopped	1 t.	3 t.
Salt to taste		

Soak fruit galaxy and onion flakes, bring to boil, add all seasonings and let simmer until fruit is done and flavors are well mixed. The mixture should be sweet-hot. The seasonings should be mixed at home and packaged with fruit galaxy, onion flakes, sugar, and ginger root.

Sambals

Raisins	4 oz.	1 lb.
Nuts, chopped	4 oz.	1 lb.
Banana flakes	4 oz.	1 lb.
Shredded coconut	2 oz.	8 oz.

When serving curry over rice, set out chutney with sambals in separate cups or heaped in mounds on a pan or lid. Each guest adds chutney and sambals to the curry.

The meal is best served on a layover day. Unused sambals can be added to breakfast cereal, or to a dessert such as cheesecake.

Macaroni and cheese with shrimp

Cream sauce (see recipe, p. 115)		
Cheddar cheese, diced	10 oz.	40 oz.
Macaroni	8 oz.	32 oz.
Dried shrimps	2 oz.	8 oz.
Salt and pepper to taste		

Prepare the cream sauce, adding the cheese after it thickens. Add the shrimps to about 2 gal. of cold water, bring to a boil, salt to taste, add the macaroni and cook for about 30 minutes. Drain and add to the sauce. If there is a shortage of pots, double the amount of water in the sauce. Cook the shrimps and macaroni in this water before adding the milk and flour mixture.

Tuna-shrimp pilaf

Water	2 qt.	2 gal.
Dried shrimps	3 oz.	12 oz.
Dried mushrooms	1/2 oz. (approx.)	2 oz.
Onion flakes	1/2 oz. (approx.)	2 oz.
Pepper flakes	1/4 oz.	1 oz.
Tomato flakes	1 oz. (1/3 cup)	4 oz. (1-1/2 c.)
Bulghour wheat (e.g., Ala)	6 oz.	30 oz.
Tarragon	1/4 t.	1 t.
Basil	1/4 t.	1 t.
Garlic powder to taste	1/4 t.	1 t.

Tuna in oil	7 oz. (1 can)	28 oz. (4 cans)
or freeze-dried tuna	2 oz.	8 oz.
Margarine	2 oz.	8 oz.
	(1/2 cube)	(2 cubes)

Salt and pepper to taste

Break mushrooms into bits, add to shrimp and soak for 10 minutes in the cold water. Add the other vegetables, bring to a boil, and add the wheat and remaining ingredients. Cook about 40 minutes or until the wheat is soft.

Creamed chipped beef

Cream sauce (see recipe p. 115)		
Chipped beef (dry type) 8 oz.	32 oz.
Parsley flakes (optional) 1 t.	1 T.

Prepare the cream sauce as directed, but *omit the salt*. Add the other ingredients to the cream sauce, heat through and serve over rice, noodles or bulghour wheat. Salt to taste if needed.

Or, use canned salmon instead of chipped beef. 15.5 oz. for five, 64 oz. for 20 persons.

Rice

Water	2-1/2 c.	2-1/2 qt.
Precooked rice or	8 oz.	32 oz.
	(2-1/2 c.)	(2-1/2 qt.)
quick brown rice	8 oz.	32 oz.
	(1-1/2 c.)	(1-1/2 qt.)
Margarine	2 oz.	8 oz.
Salt		

For precooked rice, add the margarine to the water,

salt to taste and bring to a boil. Add the rice, simmer 5 or 10 minutes. Quick brown rice requires about 40 minutes' cooking.

Clam chowder

Bacon	4 oz.	16 oz.
Water	2 qt.	2 gal.
Potato slices (dried)	4 oz.	16 oz.
Onion flakes	1/2 oz.	2 oz.
	(3 T.)	(3/4 c.)
Parsley flakes (optional)	1/2 T.	2 T.
Minced clams	15 oz. (2 cans)	45 oz. (6 cans)
Milk powder	6 oz. (2 c.)	24 oz. (2 qt.)
Salt and pepper to taste		

Dice and fry the bacon in the soup pot, add the cold water, potato slices, and boil until potatoes are tender. Add the clams, and salt to taste. Add cold water to the milk to make a thin paste and add this to the clam mixture. Heat but do not boil. Serve with crackers and margarine for a main dish.

Desserts

Fruit gelatin

Boiling water (including juice from fruit) or, if very cold stream is not available, use total liquid of only	3-1/2 c.	3-1/2 qt.
	3 c.	3 qt.
Gelatin dessert	6 oz.	24 oz.
	(2 pkg.)	(8 pkg.)
Vacuum-dried fruit	2 oz.	8 oz.

(optional) or dried fruit (optional)	3 oz.	12 oz.

Dissolve the gelatin dessert in the boiling water and set the container in a stream to chill, weighting it with a rock on the cover. Cook the fruit until soft. Drain well, measuring the juice as part of the total liquid, add to the gelatin and chill until set. Allow 1 to 2 hours for entire process. (See Item 8, page 75)

Fruit gelatin whipped with milk

Boiling water, or if very cold stream is not available, use only	3 c.	3 qt.
	2-1/2 c.	2-1/2 qt.
Gelatin dessert	6 oz. (2 pkg.)	24 oz. (8 pkg.)
Milk powder (part whole)	4 oz. (1-1/4 c.)	16 oz. (5 c.)

Prepare gelatin dessert as above. When nearly set, stir in the milk which has been made into a thick paste with cold water. Beat well and chill until set. Whole milk powder improves the flavor. Use about 1 part whole milk to 3 parts non-fat milk.

Pudding

Instant pudding	8 oz. (2 pkg.)	32 oz. (8 pkg.)
Milk powder (part whole)	4 oz. (1-1/4 c.)	16 oz. (5 c.)
Cold water	3-1/2 c.	3-1/2 qt.
Peppermint candy (optional)	2 oz.	8 oz.
Bit marshmallows (optional)	2 oz.	8 oz.

Mix the pudding and the powdered milk. Gradually add the cold water, stirring until smooth. Vanilla pudding is good with the addition of crushed peppermint candy, or with chocolate sauce. Chocolate pudding is improved by adding bit marshmallows.

Chocolate sauce

Instant cocoa mix	4 oz. (1 c.)	16 oz. (1 qt.)
Sugar	4 oz. (1/2 c.)	16 oz. (2 c.)
Water	1/2 c.	2 c.
Margarine	1 oz.	4 oz.
Salt	1/8 t.	1/2 t.

Add the water to the cocoa and sugar, stir until smooth and bring to a boil with constant stirring. Add the margarine and salt.

Cream pie

Graham cracker crust mix	1 pkg.	4 pkg.
Instant pudding	4 oz. (1 pkg.)	20 oz. (5 pkg.)
Topping mix	1 pkg.	4 pkg.

Pat crust into a 9" pie pan. Add pudding, prepared according to recipe on p. 125. Allow to set. Prepare topping mix according to recipe on package, using 3 T. of dry milk and 1/2 c. of water instead of 1/2 c. of cold milk. Spread on top of pie. Serves 6.

Snow ice cream

Snow ice cream may be made by combining seasonings and snow. It is best made in individual servings, and part of the pleasure is experimenting with various

Sample Menus for One-Week Trip

For cooking purposes, a camp day starts with dinner and ends with breakfast. Dishes that take more than average time to prepare, such as pancakes or gelatin dessert, should be planned for days when there is reasonable expectation of ample time for cooking.

	Dinner	Breakfast
First day	Clam chowder	Applesauce
	Triscuits, margarine	Rolled oats with milk and brown sugar
	Chocolate pudding with marshmallows	Grapenuts
	Coffee, tea or chocolate	Fried smoked pork shoulder
		Coffee, tea or chocolate
Second day	Vegetable soup	Orange juice
	Beef with gravy	Hashed brown potatoes
	Mashed potato	Scrambled eggs with cheddar cheese
	Fruit cocktail	Coffee, tea or chocolate
	Coffee, tea or chocolate	
Third day	Beef broth with rice	Stewed peaches
	"Fresh" vegetable salad	Wheat Hearts with raisins, milk and brown sugar
	Boston beans	Grapenuts
	Pumpernickel bread, margarine	Fried smoked pork shoulder
	Vanilla pudding with	

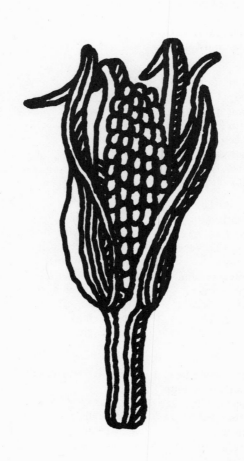

	crushed pepper- mint Coffee, tea or choco- late candy	Coffee, tea or chocolate
Fourth *day*	Cream of chicken soup Italian spaghetti with Parmesan cheese Cheesecake Coffee, tea or chocolate	Grapefruit juice Bacon Egg pancakes Syrup Coffee, tea or chocolate
Fifth *day*	Tomato soup (package mix) Corned beef hash Cabbage Applesauce and ginger snaps Coffee, tea or chocolate	Stewed prunes Wheatena with milk and brown sugar Shredded Wheat Juniors Fried smoked pork shoulder Coffee, tea or chocolate
Sixth *day*	Chicken noodle and mushroom soup Vegetable lime gel- atin salad Tamale pie Vanilla pudding with chocolate sauce	Biscuits with apricot jam Fried smoked pork shoulder Coffee, tea or chocolate

Seventh day	Green pea and onion soup	Orange juice
	Macaroni and cheese with shrimp	Grapenuts
		Bacon
	Fruit cocktail, cookies	Scrambled egg.
	Coffee, tea or chocolate	Coffee, tea or chocolate

Lunch and Snacks:

The traditional trail lunch has contained cheese, dry sausage, crackers, nuts, dried fruit, and hard candy or chocolate — foods easily carried in a cloth or plastic bag.

Cheese. For small groups, hard cheeses in red-wrapped waxed balls are a convenient size. There is also a 1-pound longhorn roll in wax which keeps well. For larger groups, cheeses such as tybo, norbo, and hard jack may be purchased in larger blocks and cut to the required size for a day's lunch for the group. If it is necessary that the cheeses keep longer than a week, cover the cut surfaces with cheesecloth and dip in hot paraffin.

Meat. Dry sausages and jerky keep best. For weekend outings or longer trips for smaller groups, 2 oz. cans of liver pate and deviled ham, key opened, are among the many kinds of meat to be found on market shelves. There are also good freeze-dried salads to be mixed at the lunch spot by adding water to the plastic bag, and letting it soak until the mixture will spread on bread or crackers. Ethnic markets offer a variety of dried meat and fish.

Bread. Hard crackers *only*, hardtack or pilot crackers, cocktail rye or pumpernickel bread, or bagels will survive best. Buy bread or crackers in compact packages — avoid the larger boxes or packages with more air space and less food.

Nuts. The choice varies from macadamia, cashew and other expensive nuts to mixed varieties and peanuts which can be purchased in markets and dime stores in every part of the country. Be sure the nuts are not rancid if you buy from bulk suppliers. There are also canned mixtures to be found.

Candy. Hard, fruit-flavored candies, preferably wrapped in paper, not foil, vary widely in quality and cost. Many imported varieties are available, but do test before you buy in any quantity. Many are priced right, attractively colored, labeled and wrapped, but lack flavor. A more expensive, more flavorful candy may be a better choice than a less expensive but flavorless one which won't be eaten.

Hard chocolate, sweet or semi-sweet, is better in cold weather. Try semi-sweet baking chocolate, in individually wrapped squares in 8-oz. packages.

Dried Fruit. This is one of the most popular lunch items. Buy fruits without sulphur when possible.

Trail Snacks. A small plastic bag of broken pieces of jerky and a wrapped square of chocolate or some hard candies is a useful pocket-size trail snack. Powdered milk mixed in a cup at a stream-crossing is also satisfying.

With a pilot cracker and some jerky, it's a satisfying light lunch.

Fruit Drinks. Fruit juice crystals used for breakfast may also be packaged for lunch, if there's too much sugar in the usual packaged fruit mix. Packaged fruit drinks are available in a wide variety of flavors. Plan for at least 3 packages per person per week, and distribute them at the roadhead so each person can mix his own when he wants it. Mix a container of juice upon arriving in camp on a hot afternoon.

Seasonings and Other Suggestions

Gourmet cooking is a relative term among camp cooks. To season or not to season is widely debated, but it is well known that any seasoning added to dehydrated or freeze-dried foods will improve the product. With a bit of imagination, some interesting and tasty meals can be prepared. Here are some suggestions:

Soup: The cook may start with some bouillon cubes, and the pint of water per person usually considered an adequate amount of soup. After that, almost anything goes.

1. Add 1/2 oz. of celery flakes per package of onion soup and simmer until flakes are cooked. Top each serving with Parmesan cheese, as is done with onion soup.

2. Chicken broth thickened with 1 tablespoon instant potato powder and 1 tablespoon dry milk per pint of liquid, seasoned with 1 teaspoon dill weed,

makes a good potato soup. If beef broth is used, simmer dill seed in the beef-potato soup.

3. Dehydrated vegetables, with either beef or chicken bouillon and the cook's choice of herb seasonings, is quick and easy. Add a few drops of sherry just before serving.

4. Packaged pea soup is more interesting with thyme to taste, and a few small rounds of fried chorizo (Mexican sausage) or bits of ham left from lunch. Dice the meat into the soup when the pot is put on the fire, so its smoky flavor blends into the soup.

5. Add green noodles to any bouillon pot or meat stew for a colorful touch. They are colored with spinach. Red noodles are made with beet juice.

6. Bagels are good dipped into soup, or cut in thin rounds, tossed in butter and garlic powder as a crouton to add to soup or salad.

Main Course. For better flavor, add seasonings to freeze-dried or dehydrated meat and vegetables while soaking. Try these variations to the recipes on other pages:

1. Bring a pint of red wine in a plastic bottle and add to the water used to reconstitute beef. Use white wine for chicken or turkey.

2. Buy canned hams in 1 or 3 lb. sizes. Juices and fat will be part of the net weight, so be generous in planning the amount per person. Ham not used for dinner can be sliced thin for lunch, or chopped into the breakfast eggs.

Bake the ham with this seasoning: Mix at home 3 tablespoons dry mustard, 3 tablespoons sherry, 3 table-spoons apple or guava jelly for each 3 lb. can of ham.

Jerky: The word comes from the Spanish *Charqui* or dried meat. Indians prepared it from venison, horse, buffalo, and other animals. Venison is a good meat for jerky as it contains little fat.

Jerky may be purchased in many markets, but you can make your own. Take 2 pounds of top or bottom round, or sirloin tip steak 1/2" to 3/4" thick. Cut off fat and gristle. Slice into 1/2" thick strips with the grain. Season with salt — pepper or garlic powder are optional. Lay meat on an oven broiler rack and place in the oven, or on the upturned wire rack of an electric roaster. Set the oven as low as possible, about 210° and dry the meat for 10 or 12 hours, or longer if necessary. If an electric roaster is used, set at about 210° with lid open about 1" and dry slowly for 24 hours or until meat is completely dry and crisp. It must dry *very slowly*. The meat will dry to about 1/3 of its original weight. It will be crisp and will keep well for several months. The less fat, the longer it will keep for the fat becomes rancid after a few weeks.

The meat is good for breakfast, for lunch, or added to soup or stew for dinner.

Some Edible Wild Plants

Many wild plants may be easily identified and used to supplement the hiker's diet. Some common plants to be found along the trail are blackberries, blueberries, raspberries, strawberries, and rose hips. The hip is the seed pod of the rose. It may be dried and used for a hot drink, or eaten as a trail snack.

The young leaves of wild mustard, dandelion, lamb's quarter (wild spinach) or miner's lettuce and watercress are good either cooked or raw. An old favorite dressing for raw greens (or lettuce) is to fry three or four pieces of bacon crisp, remove from the pan and break into bits over the greens. There should be at least one cup of greens per person. To the pan's 3 or 4 tbsp. of bacon fat, add an equal amount of vinegar. Cook briefly and pour over the greens. The salad may also contain a chopped boiled egg or two, and a few chopped wild onions.

The same dressing may be poured over boiled greens. The greens should be cooked in a very small amount of water until wilted but not overcooked.

Wild onions may be found in all parts of the country. They are easily identified by the long tubular leaves and onion smell. Look in meadows and along streams for them. Eat them raw as a trail snack, or chop into salads, vegetables, soups or stews.

Watercress may be added to potato soup, or used to garnish any dish. Any of the wild greens may be added to lettuce salads.

Pennyroyal and other wild mints are delicious added to hot or cold tea, or to stronger beverages such as Mountain Mint Juleps.

Pine nuts are good roasted as a tasty addition to lunch or to soup. Rich in protein, they were widely used by the Indians.

Eat *no* mushrooms or other fungi unless you are sure it's the non-poisonous variety.

There are many books with excellent descriptions, photos and drawings of edible plants, and one should become knowledgeable about plants before foraging too widely afield. Check the bookstores and libraries for expert advice. Wild foods are not in large supply in most places, but small amounts are fun to try.

Cooking Equipment Lists

The following lists of cooking equipment are suitable for preparing any of the recipes given, if proper care is taken to plan menus in advance. If only three cooking pots and one plastic mixing bowl are carried, main dishes will need to be prepared in one pot and water for beverages cannot be heated until the soup pot is empty, unless dessert is in the mixing bowl.

Four pots are a great convenience especially if the water supply is far from camp.

All handles should be of wood or metal. Plastic is apt to melt.

Cooking equipment for a party of five

	Approximate weight
Light-weight wire grill (8″ x 12″)	6 oz.
Nested light-weight aluminum saucepans (2, 2-1/2 and 3 qt.), covers, cake pan (9″) and pot grabber: or	
Set of light-weight nested pots with frying pan covers	3 lbs.
Plastic mixing bowl (about 2 qts.) or shaker (1 qt.)	4 oz.
2 mixing spoons	
1 light spatula	
1 paring knife (if no pocket knife)	
1 wire whip (optional)	10 oz.
1 can opener (if needed)	
1 metal or hard plastic sponge	
1 extra cup	
1 pair canvas work gloves	
1 pair pliers	

Plastic or light-weight cloth
  bag for pots

	2 oz.
4 lbs.	6 oz.

Cooking equipment for a party of twenty

	Approximate weight
Wire grill (11″ x 17″)	2 lbs.
1 pot, 1 gallon, with cover	
1 pot, 2 gallon, with cover	9 lbs. 6 oz.
2 pots, 3-1/2 gallon, with covers	
Aluminum griddle (10″ x 17″)	2 lbs.
Plastic dishpan for mixing	12 oz.
Pot grabber or pliers	
Can opener (if needed)	
2 ladles (1 cup capacity)	
1 wire whisk	
2 large stirring spoons	
1 tablespoon	4 lbs. 2 oz.
1 teaspoon	
1 spatula	
1 long-handled brush	
1 oven mitt	
1 pair work gloves	
1 metal sponge	
Plastic sheet, about 9′ x 12′	12 oz.
Cloth bags for pots	1 lb.
	20 lbs.

Partial List of Suppliers for Light-Weight Foods

The boom in freeze-dried and dehydrated foods is bringing more and more kinds of these lightweight items to supermarket shelves. Check your local markets, health food stores and the gourmet sections of department stores.

Some suppliers specializing in lightweight foods are listed below. Some offer more variety than others. Ask for catalogs and learn which foods are available.

Ace Sporting Goods Co., Denver, Colorado

Antelope Camping and Equipment Co., 10268 Imperial Ave., Cupertino, Calif.

Chuck Wagon Foods, 175 Oak St., Newton, Mass. 02164

Camp and Trail, 21 Park Place, New York, N.Y. 10007

Cloud Cap Chalet, 1127 S.W. Morrison Ave., Portland, Ore.

Dagna's Market, 1382 Solano, Albany, Calif. 94706

Dri-Lite Foods, 11333 Atlantic, Lynwood, Calif. 90264

Family Market, 1301 I Street, Anchorage, Alaska 99501

Gary King Sporting Goods, 1231 West Northern Lights Blvd., Anchorage, Alaska 99501

Gerry Mountaineering Equipment Co., Ward, Colorado

S. Gumpert Co., Inc.
   812 Jersey Avenue, Jersey City, N.J. 07302
   425 E. Illinois Street, Chicago, Ill. 60611
   3915 Capitol Ave., Houston, Texas 77023

H & H Surplus Center, 1104 W. Baltimore St., Baltimore Md. 21223

Hickory Farms of Ohio, P.O. Box 3306, Van Nuys, Calif. (also Mill Valley, San Anselmo, Palo Alto, and San Jose, Calif.; and Honolulu, Hawaii)

Holiday Brand Concentrated Foods, P.O. Box 47, Glendale, Calif.

Holubar Mountaineering Ltd., 1975 30th Street, Boulder, Colorado

Ken's Light Pack, 1205 Laurel Street, San Carlos, Calif.

Leon Greenman, 132 Spring Street, New York, New York 10012

Perma Pak, 40 East 2430 St., Salt Lake City, Utah

Recreational Equipment, Inc., 1525 11th Ave., Seattle, Wash. 98122

Rich-Moor Corporation P.O. Box 2728, Van Nuys, Calif. 91404; 616 N. Robertson Blvd., Los Angeles, Calif. 90069

Spiro's, Town & Country Village, Palo Alto, Calif.

Stow-a-Way Products Co., Inc., 103 Ripley Road, Cohasset, Mass. 02025

The Mountain Shop
228 Grant Avenue, San Francisco, Calif. 94108
1028 Sir Francis Drake Blvd., Kentfield, Calif. 94965

The Ski Hut, 1615 University Ave., Berkeley, Calif.

The Smilie Company, 575 Howard St., San Francisco Calif. 94105

The Sports Chalet, 906 W. Northern Lights Blvd. Anchorage, Alaska 99501

The Army and Navy Surplus, Roswell, New Mexico

Trail Chef, 1109 S. Wall Street, Los Angeles, Calif. 90015